ENGLISCH FÜR KINDER

READ ENGLISH WITH ZIGZAG -3

Copyright © 2022 Zigzag English / Lydia Winter

All rights reserved. No part of this publication may be reproduced or transmitted in any form without the written permission of the author.

ISBN: 978-1-914911-20-0

www.zigzagenglish.co.uk

www.zigzagenglish.co.uk – BOOKS FOR ENGLISH LEARNERS

OUR BOOKS FOR CHILDREN

Our bilingual picture books for younger children. *Funny stories in simple, useful everyday English, with colour photos.*
English with Tony -1- Tony moves house
English with Tony -2- Tony is happy
English with Tony -3- Tony's Christmas
English with Tony -4- Tony's holiday
My best friend

Our coursebook for beginners *(age 7 to 11)*
English for Children - 1st Coursebook *(Essential vocabulary and grammar for beginners)*

Our dialogue books for beginners *(age 7 to 11).*
I Speak English Too! - 1
I Speak English Too! - 2

Our series of reading and comprehension books for beginners *(age 7 to 11).*
Read English with Zigzag - 1
Read English with Zigzag - 2
Read English with Zigzag - 3
   Audiobook at Audible.com

Our vocabulary book with photos, word puzzles and more *(age 7+)*
300+ mots en anglais / 300+ englische Wörter / 300+ palabras en inglés / 300+ parole inglesi

The Learn English Activity Book for Children *(A1 - A2, elementary). (Recommended for children in early secondary school.)*

Our series of reading and comprehension books for children at elementary level *(A1 - A2) (recommended for ages 10 to 13). With lots of language activities.*
Read English with Ben - 1
Read English with Ben - 2
Read English with Ben - 3

Our YOU DECIDE adventure book with 1 beginning and 19 endings. A2
(11+) Your Bilingual Fairy Tale Adventure

Our series of reading and discussion books about a family with superpowers (with writing tasks) for children at secondary school, A2 - B1
I Live in a Castle – Book 1 – My Superpower
I Live in a Castle – Book 2 – The New Me

The Speak English, Read English, Write English Activity Books – *3 books from A1 to B2, for older children and adults.*

Our non-fiction book with language activities
Learn English with Fun Facts! – A2 - B2

English Dialogues for Teenagers – for ages 11 to 17, A2 - B2

OUR BOOKS FOR ADULTS

Our 3 Grammar books with grammar-focused dialogues
Learn English Grammar through Conversation – A1, A2 and B1

Our Dialogue books for adults (with vocabulary lists and comprehension questions). Audiobooks are available for some of these books – at Audible.com.
50 very Easy Everyday English Dialogues (A2)
50 Easy Everyday English Dialogues (A2 - B1)
50 Intermediate Everyday English Dialogues (B1 - B2)
50 more Intermediate Everyday English Dialogues (B1 - B2)
40 Advanced Everyday English Dialogues (B2 - C1)
40 Intermediate Business English Dialogues (B1 - B2)
40 Advanced Business English Dialogues (B2 - C1)

Our activity books for adults and older children
The Speak English, Read English, Write English Activity Books – 3 books, for A1 - A2, A2 - B1 and B1 - B2.

Our non-fiction book with language activities
Learn English with Fun Facts! – A2 - B2

Contents

- Die Ziele dieser Buchreihe sind: 5
- Wie Sie diese Buchreihe verwenden können: 5
- Was noch? Wie geht es weiter? 5
- 1 I'm not a cat 7
- 2 One or two things you need to know 8
- 3 Dogs are better than cats 9
- 4 Big, bigger, biggest 10
- 5 A long time ago 11
- 6 Old enough 13
- 7 A very brave thing 15
- 8 At school 18
- 9 Something interesting 19
- 10 Goldilocks and the 3 bears 21
- 11 Cat in a tree 24
- 12 Terrible danger 26
- 13 Dogs can't climb trees 29
- 14 The school rules 31
- 15 The plan 33
- 16 Lunch 35
- 17 A lazy cat 37
- 18 Animal tracks 38
- 19 Bad dog! 39
- Find the opposites. 42
- What are the words? 42
  - Antworten: 43
  - Vielen Dank, dass Sie dieses Buch gelesen haben. 45
  - From: I Speak English Too! - 2 46
  - From: Read English with Ben - 1 47
  - From: The Learn English Activity Book 48

Die Ziele dieser Buchreihe sind:

1. Eine unterhaltsame und lustige Lektüre zu sein.
2. Ihrem Kind das Vertrauen zu geben, Englisch zu lesen.
3. Ihrem Kind Schlüsselwörter und -sätze beizubringen. Die Bücher führen diese ein, wiederholen sie und bauen sie nach und nach auf, um das Verständnis Ihres Kindes für die englische Sprache zu erweitern.
4. Ihrem Kind auf einfache Weise die Grundlagen in englischer Grammatik beizubringen.

Wie Sie diese Buchreihe verwenden können:

1. Vielleicht kann Ihr Kind die Bücher schon ohne Hilfe lesen. Das ist großartig! Aber wenn Sie Englisch sprechen, können Sie ihm bei der Aussprache helfen, indem Sie es ermutigen, Ihnen einige Kapitel laut vorzulesen. **Die Bücher 1 und 2 sind auch als Hörbuch erhältlich.**
2. In jedem Buch gibt es Vokabellisten, die Sie verwenden können, um Ihrem Kind beim Lernen der neuen Wörter zu helfen.
3. Es gibt Verständnisfragen, mit Antworten am Ende jedes Buches. Sie können natürlich weitere Fragen hinzufügen und Gespräche über die Geschichte führen.
4. Es gibt weitere sprachliche Aktivitäten, die Ihrem Kind beim Erlernen von Wortschatz und Grammatik helfen.

Was noch? Wie geht es weiter?

1. Unsere Reihe mit einfachen Dialogen - **I Speak English Too!** - ist für Eltern gedacht, die ihrem Kind helfen wollen, Englisch zu sprechen. Sie ist ideal für Eltern und Kind, oder für zwei Kinder die gemeinsam lesen und sprechen möchten. Buch 1 beginnt mit den Grundlagen, indem es Schlüsselwörter und -sätze einführt und dann vertieft, sodass Ihr Kind schnelle Fortschritte macht. Schon nach wenigen Lektionen wird Ihr Kind kleine Dialoge auf Englisch mit Ihnen führen können.
2. Das Lesen von Büchern auf Englisch - egal wie einfach sie sind - macht einen großen Unterschied. Wir empfehlen auch, einfache Fernsehserien für Kinder anzuschauen. Auch wenn sie für englische Muttersprachler konzipiert sind, die etwas jünger sind als Ihr Kind. Auch Hörbücher eignen sich hervorragend, vor allem kurz vor dem Schlafengehen (das hilft dem Kind, die neue Sprache zu beizubehalten). Erwarten Sie nicht, dass Ihr Kind alles sofort versteht - Hörbücher können

immer wieder angehört werden, und Ihr Kind wird jedes Mal mehr verstehen.
3.   Es ist aufregend zu sehen, wie schnell Ihr Kind Fortschritte in einer neuen Sprache macht. Viel Glück und viel Spaß!

From wolf to pet

1 I'm not a cat

Oh, look at all those children. Hello, children! I'm your friend! Can I **wash** your **face** for you? Is that okay? Can we go for a walk? Can I take my ball? Can you **throw** the ball for me?

What's that? What did you say?

I'm not Zigzag, no. I'm not a cat. I'm not a tiger. Do I look like a cat or a tiger?

No, I don't. I look like a dog. That's because I AM A DOG.

I'm a beautiful, big, black and white dog. I'm white with black spots. I'm a dalmatian dog.

Do you know my name? Do you remember who I am?

That's right. I'm Pam!

Vocabulary:
- to wash   waschen
- face   Gesicht
- to throw   werfen

2 One or two things you need to know

If you have a dog:

1. You have to take your dog for a walk every morning.

2. You have to take your dog for a walk every evening.

3. Do NOT **forget** to take your dog for a walk!

Vocabulary:
- to forget   vergessen

3 Dogs are better than cats

I'm Pam. I'm not Zigzag, I'm Pam.

Sorry about that.

No, I'm not sorry. I'm not sorry - I'm **happy**. I'm happy, because - guess what? I'm **better** than Zigzag.

I'm a dog, and Zigzag is a cat. Zigzag is NOT A TIGER. He's a cat.

Dogs are better than cats. So - I'm better than Zigzag. **Right?**

I'm bigger than Zigzag. I'm nicer than Zigzag. I'm more beautiful than Zigzag. I'm more intelligent than Zigzag. I like children more than Zigzag does.

And this is my book. It's not Zigzag's book - it's mine!

Vocabulary:
- happy   glücklich
- better   besser
- right?   oder?

4 Big, bigger, biggest

This is a small dog. It's not very big. It's the smallest dog.

This is a bigger dog. It's quite big.

This dog is even bigger. It's the biggest dog. It's really very big. It's enormous.

5 A long time ago

Some dogs are big and some dogs are small. Some dogs have long **ears** and some dogs have short **tails**. Some dogs are brown and some dogs are white with black spots **like** me.

Some dogs...

Okay, you know what I mean. All dogs are **different**.

But a very, very, very, very, very long time ago, all dogs were the same. That's right - all dogs were:

WOLVES!!

Wolves are enormous. Wolves have **sharp teeth**. Wolves are really scary. But most of all, wolves are **BRAVE**.

A long time ago, I was a wolf. Now, I'm a dog and I live in Adam and Poppy's house with Zigzag the cat.

But I'm still brave.

Vocabulary:
- a long time ago   vor langer Zeit
- ear   Ohr
- tail   Schwanz
- like   wie
- different   anders
- sharp   scharf
- tooth   Zahn
- brave   mutig

6 Old enough

Adam is four years **younger** than Poppy. When Adam was a baby, Poppy was **already** at school. When Adam **learned** to talk, Poppy learned to read. When Adam learned to walk, Poppy learned to run races.

Then Adam went to nursery with the other very small children and **painted** pictures with his hands. And Poppy started to **write stories**.

But now, **at last**, Adam's old enough to go to school with Poppy.

On his first day at school, Adam was excited. He really wanted to go to school. He didn't want to be little. He wanted to be a big boy.

He walked to school with Mum and with Poppy and her best friend Jessica. He wore his **own** school uniform – black trousers and a red top. He had his own red **book bag**. He felt **proud**. He **felt** a little bit scared.

Questions:
1. How much older than Adam is Poppy?
2. How did Adam feel about starting school?
3. Why was his book bag red?

Vocabulary:
- younger   jünger
- already   bereits
- to learn   lernen
- to paint   malen

- to write — schreiben
- story — Geschichte
- at last — endlich
- own — eigene
- book bag — Büchertasche
- proud — stolz
- to feel — fühlen

7 A very brave thing

This summer, I did a very brave thing. I did the bravest thing a dog can do.

We all went for a picnic. Well, not Zigzag, because he's a cat. Cats have to stay at home.

There was a river. Mum and Dad and Poppy and I can swim. But Adam can't swim. He's too young.

Adam was in **danger**. Mum and Dad and Poppy were there. But they didn't **see** the danger.

I saw the danger. I saw Adam run and fall into the water. I jumped into the water. It was **deep**. It was too deep for me.

I swam to Adam. He put his arms round my **neck**. I **pulled** him out of the water.

Everyone said "Good dog! Brave dog!"

I'm a big, strong, brave dog and I **saved** Adam.

Vocabulary:
- danger   Gefahr
- to see   sehen

- deep   tief
- neck   Hals
- to pull   ziehen
- to save   retten

8 At school

At school, there were so many children. There were hundreds of them. **Nearly all** of them were older and bigger than Adam. Because it was Adam's first day, Mum was there. She took a photo of Adam in front of the school. And then she went into the classroom with Adam. Adam wanted Mum to stay with him. He started to **cry**. But Mum said goodbye, and she **left**.

Adam looked at all the other boys and girls in his class. There were lots and lots of them. He **only** knew one of them. Billy, from nursery. Adam didn't like Billy, and Billy didn't like Adam. "Hello, Billy," said Adam. Billy said **nothing**.

Adam sat on the **floor** with all the other children. The teacher told a story. It was the story of Goldilocks and the Three Bears.

Questions:
1. Why did mum go into the classroom with Adam?
2. Was Adam happy to be at school?
3. Why didn't Billy talk to Adam?

Vocabulary:
- nearly — fast
- all — alle
- to cry — weinen
- to leave — verlassen
- only — nur
- nothing — nichts
- floor — Boden

9 Something interesting

Adam went to school today. It was very quiet here without him.

Mum and dad were **out**. Poppy and Adam were at school. Only Zigzag was here. I like Zigzag, but he's **just** a cat. He doesn't understand much. He went to school with Poppy once, but I don't think he learned **anything**.

I went into the garden. I watched Zigzag **catch** a spider. I watched Zigzag eat the spider. Zigzag said it was delicious. I looked for a spider, but I couldn't find one.

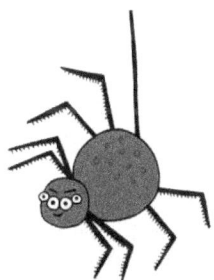

Then I saw something interesting. Something very interesting. The next door neighbour's white cat was in the next door neighbour's garden.

I did a bad thing. I knew it was a bad thing, but I did it.

I **barked** at the cat – WOOF WOOF! Then I jumped over the **fence** into the next door neighbour's garden. The cat ran. I chased her. I chased her round and round the garden and up the neighbour's tree. She sat in the tree and looked at me.

Vocabulary:
- out   aus
- just   nur
- he didn't learn anything   er hat nichts gelernt
- to catch   fangen
- to bark   bellen
- fence   Zaun

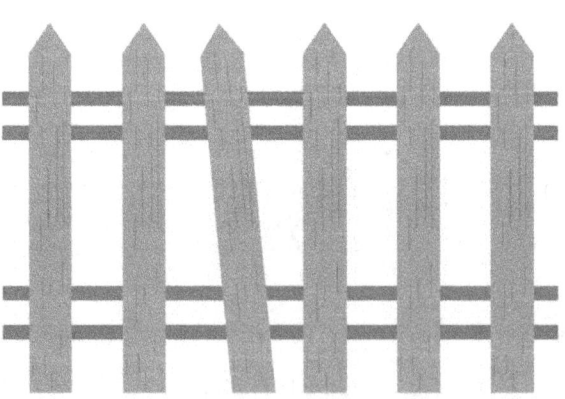

10 Goldilocks and the 3 bears

Goldilocks was a girl with gold hair (really?) who went into the **forest**, looking for some breakfast.

She found it in a bears' house (do bears live in houses?) and ate it.

Luckily for Goldilocks, the bears were out. Bears are extremely big and strong and sometimes eat little girls.

Then Goldilocks sat on a little chair and **broke** it.

She was tired, so she went upstairs to the bedroom and went to sleep on Baby Bear's bed.

When the three bears got **back** home, they were hungry. They wanted to eat their breakfast, but it was gone. Baby Bear wanted to sit on his chair, but it was broken. When they found Goldilocks on Baby Bear's bed, Father Bear wanted to eat her, but Baby Bear wanted to play with her.

Goldilocks **woke up**. She was scared. She jumped out of the window and ran home. She never went into the forest again.

Questions:
  1. Why did Goldilocks go into the forest?
  2. Were the bears at home?
  3. Did Baby Bear want to eat Goldilocks?

Vocabulary:
- forest — Wald
- to break — zerbrechen
- back — zurück
- to wake up — aufwachen

11 Cat in a tree

The white cat sat in the tree. It sat in the tree for five long minutes.

I wanted that cat. I don't know why I wanted her, but I did.

Zigzag is a cat, and I don't chase Zigzag. But Zigzag is family. I chase every other cat. All dogs chase cats. It's what we do.

But I had a problem. Cats can **climb** trees. Dogs can't climb trees. The white cat was in a tree. I needed to go **up**, or I needed the cat to come **down**.

I tried to climb the tree. I really, really **tried**. But it was no good. I'm big, strong, brave and intelligent, but I can't climb.

I **asked** the cat to come down. I said I wanted to talk to her. I was very **polite**. She was polite too, but she said no. She didn't want to come down. She was comfortable in the tree. It was nice up there.

I wanted that cat.

Vocabulary:
- to climb — klettern
- up — rauf
- down — runter
- to try — versuchen
- to ask — bitten
- polite — höflich

12 Terrible danger

Adam **listened** to the story, but he didn't like it. It was scary.

The teacher showed the children a picture of Goldilocks. She was a very small girl. Then the teacher showed them a picture of the three bears. Baby Bear was quite **cute**, but Mother Bear was enormous and Father Bear was the biggest bear **ever**.

Adam knew Goldilocks was in **terrible** danger. **If** the bears came home and found Goldilocks in their house, they would **probably** eat her. If she tried to run away, they would chase her and catch her. **Then** they would eat her.

When the teacher read that Goldilocks climbed onto Baby Bear's bed and went to sleep, Adam **jumped up** and **shouted**: "Don't go to sleep, Goldilocks! **Run away**! The bears are coming!" The teacher looked at Adam and told him to sit down and be quiet.

Father Bear didn't eat Goldilocks. But he very nearly did, thought Adam.

Questions:
 1. *Which bear was the biggest?*
 2. *What did Baby Bear look like?*
 3. *What was the most dangerous thing Goldilocks did?*

Vocabulary:

- to listen — zuhören
- cute — süß
- ever — aller Zeiten
- terrible — schrecklich
- if — wenn
- probably — wahrscheinlich
- then — dann
- to jump up — aufspringen
- to shout — schreien
- to run away — weglaufen

13 Dogs can't climb trees

Do you know what I **decided** to do?

Dogs can't climb trees. That was the problem. Dogs can't climb trees, but cats can. So the white cat was in the tree, and I was under the tree. The cat was safe. Or was she?

It was **simple**, really.

Most cats are my **enemies**. But one is my friend. That's right – Zigzag is my friend, my family.

I jumped back over the fence into my garden and looked for Zigzag. He was where he **usually** is. He was on the sofa in the living room, sleeping.

I bit his tail just a little bit, to wake him up. He wasn't happy. He **hissed** at me.

I **explained** my problem with the white cat.

"Please help me, Zigzag," I said.

"Okay," said Zigzag. "But only if you **give** me what I want".

Maybe he's more intelligent than I thought.

Vocabulary:
- to decide   entscheiden
- simple   einfach
- most   die meisten
- enemy   Feind
- usually   normalerweise
- to hiss   zischen
- to explain   erklären
- to give   geben

14 The school rules

After the story, Adam's class went into the school **hall** - the biggest room in the school. All the other children in the school were already there, sitting on the floor.

The Headteacher **welcomed** the new children in Adam's class to the school. Then everyone **stood up** and sang a **song**. Adam didn't **know** what to sing, but he tried to **copy** the others.

After that, the Headteacher read the school **rules**:
1. Get to school on time.
2. Listen to the teacher.
3. Put your hand up if you want to ask a question.
4. Always **try hard**.
5. Don't **waste time**.
6. Be **kind** and polite.

Adam was **worried**. He wanted to ask a question, but he was too scared to put his hand up.

If a child broke a rule, was there a **punishment**?

Questions:
1. *What was the biggest room in the school called?*
2. *Which school rule do you think is the most important?*
3. *If you break a school rule at your school, is there a punishment?*

Vocabulary:
- hall — Saal
- to welcome — begrüßen
- to stand up — aufstehen
- song — Lied
- to know — wissen
- to copy — kopieren
- rule — Regel
- to try hard — sich anstrengen
- to waste time — Zeit verschwenden
- kind — freundlich
- worried — besorgt
- punishment — Strafe

15 The plan

This was the plan. It wasn't **difficult**. In fact, I thought it was very easy.

Zigzag is much bigger than the white cat. He just had to climb the tree and chase the white cat down to me. Simple.

But first, I had to do something for Zigzag.

Poor Zigzag. Because he's just a cat, he can't do much. He can't open the kitchen door. He can't open the fridge door. He can't take the cat food out of the fridge.

Zigzag hates waiting for dinner time. So he **often** asks me to give him his cat food. I **always** say no. Zigzag eats too much. **More** food isn't good for him.

But I really, really wanted that white cat. So, just this **once**, I opened the kitchen door and opened the fridge door. I took the cat food out of the fridge.

Zigzag ate some cat food. "I'm tired now," he said. "I want to go to sleep on my sofa".

"Oh no." I said. "Now you have to do what I want. Climb that tree!"

Vocabulary:
- difficult   schwierig
- often   oft
- always   immer
- more   mehr
- once   einmal

16 Lunch

Adam was hungry. When he went to nursery, he had a snack at eleven o'clock every morning. Today, he had to wait **until** lunchtime at half past twelve.

He played with sand and water and balls. He painted a picture of his cat and dog. He looked at the picture books in the big **bookcase**. He tried to write his name with a **pencil**.

And at last it was lunchtime. Some children had **packed lunches** from home in beautiful lunchboxes. They ate their sandwiches outside in the **playground**. But Adam went to the big hall again. This time, it was **full** of tables and chairs. He **queued** up for his food and sat down at a table next to a boy from his class. Lunch was chicken with **mashed potato** and **peas**. With strawberry ice cream for **pudding**. It wasn't delicious, but it wasn't too bad.

After lunch, Adam and his new friend ran outside. Adam saw Poppy playing football with the **older** boys and girls. He started to **enjoy** school.

Questions:
1. What was the most fun thing that Adam did?
2. What do you think of Adam's school lunch? Was it like your school lunches?

Vocabulary:
- until — bis
- bookcase — Bücherregal
- pencil — Bleistift
- packed lunch — Lunchpaket
- playground — Schulhof
- full — voll
- to queue — anstehen
- mashed potato — Kartoffelpüree
- pea — Erbse
- older — älter
- to enjoy — Genießen

17 A lazy cat

Zigzag wasn't happy. He's a lazy cat. To be honest, he's an extremely lazy cat. He never wants to help people. He never wants to help other animals. He only thinks about himself. It's not really his fault. He's just a cat.

He walked into the garden. Very slowly. He jumped onto the garden fence. He jumped down into the neighbour's garden. He looked up at the tree. The white cat looked down at him. She stayed exactly where she was.

Then Zigzag ran at the tree. He jumped. And he fell. He fell back down. Zigzag is a big cat. He's a fat cat. I don't think he's very good at climbing trees.

Zigzag looked at me. "You ate the cat food." I said. "Now climb the tree!" Zigzag tried again. This time he **made it**. He was in the tree. But where was the white cat?

Vocabulary:
- to make it   es schaffen

18 Animal tracks

Look out for animal tracks in your garden or park. You can find them in snow or mud.

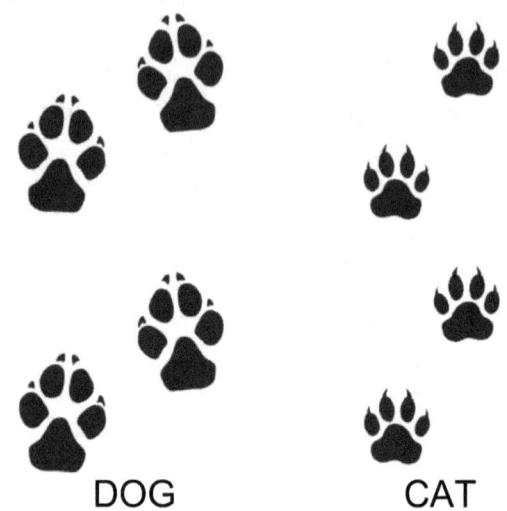

DOG   CAT

Watch out for bears – they're dangerous!

19 Bad dog!

The white cat was at the **top** of the tree. She was at the end of a thin branch.

"Go on, Zigzag! Chase that cat down!"

Zigzag slowly climbed up the tree. He climbed higher and higher. He climbed onto the white cat's branch. He was **almost** there.

CRACK!!

The branch broke. Zigzag fell down. The white cat fell down. I saw her and she saw me. She ran and I ran. I chased that cat round the garden. I chased her round the garden again. I chased her onto the **street**. I chased her down the street.

"Pam! **Stop!** Bad dog!"

Adam? Adam and Poppy and Mum? Back from school already? Where's the white cat? Oh no. She's up **another** tree. I WANT THAT CAT!

"Oh Pam", said Adam. "I had such a great time at school today."

Vocabulary:
- top — Spitze
- almost — fast
- street — Straße
- stop! — halt!
- another — ein anderer

Find the opposites.

up	go
never	in
bad	different
the same	wake up
out	noisy
stop	dangerous
quiet	down
easy	good
cute	always
safe	scary
go to sleep	difficult

What are the words?

Adam is alm-st five. He's very y-ung, but he's a pol-t- child. He al-ays says thank you.

My dad says English is quite e-sy. But I'm ter-ibl- at it!

Your English is b-t-er than my English.

Please read me the -tor- of Goldilocks and the Three Bears. – In a m-n-te!

Antworten:

6
1. She's four years older than Adam.
2. He felt excited, scared and a little bit proud. He really wanted to go to school.
3. Because his school uniform was red.

8
1. Because it was his first day at school.
2. No, he wasn't happy. He didn't want his mum to leave.
3. Because he didn't like him.

10
1. She went into the forest to find some breakfast.
2. No, they weren't; they were out.
3. No, he didn't want to eat her. He wanted to play with her.

12
1. Father Bear was the biggest.
2. He looked quite cute.
3. The most dangerous thing she did was to go to sleep on Baby Bear's bed.

14
1. It was called the school hall.
2. You decide.

16
1. You decide.
2. You decide.

up	down
never	always
bad	good
the same	different
out	in
stop	go
quiet	noisy
easy	difficult
cute	scary
safe	dangerous
go to sleep	wake up

Adam is almost five. He's very young, but he's a polite child. He always says thank you.

My dad says English is quite easy. But I'm terrible at it!

Your English is better than my English.

Please read me the story of Goldilocks and the Three Bears. – In a minute!

Vielen Dank, dass Sie dieses Buch gelesen haben.

Wenn Sie Fragen oder Vorschläge zur Verbesserung des Buches haben, schicken Sie mir bitte eine E-Mail an: lydiawinter.zigzagenglish@gmail.com. Vorschläge für neue Bücher sind auch immer willkommen.

Die Website finden Sie hier: **www.zigzagenglish.co.uk**. Auf dieser Website können Sie und Ihr Kind sich über unsere anderen Bücher für Kinder und Erwachsene informieren und unseren Blog lesen. Sie finden dort auch weitere englischsprachige Aktivitäten.

Ich würde mich freuen, wenn Sie eine Buchrezension hinterlassen. Vielen Dank!

Hier sind einige Auszüge aus unseren anderen Büchern für Kinder, die anfangen, Englisch zu lernen:

From: I Speak English Too! - 2

8A: A week's holiday

Katie: It's my **half term** holiday next week. A **whole** week with no school!

Anna: Are you going **away**?

Katie: Yes. We're going to the Lake District.

Anna: What's that? Where is it?

Katie: It's in the **north** of England. There are lots of **mountains** and **lakes**. It's very beautiful.

Anna: Lucky you! I have school next week.

Katie: School is really hard at the moment. I'm tired. I need a **break**.

Anna: Is your whole family going?

Katie: No. My mum has to work next week. So she's **staying** at home.

Anna: Your **poor** mum.

From: Read English with Ben - 1

14. Present

The day after the last day of school was the first day of the summer holidays. But Ben didn't feel excited. He felt unhappy.

He **lay** on his bed in his bedroom with a book. But he didn't read the book. He thought about all those years at primary school. He thought about his friends.

His mum **called** him. "It's lunchtime, Ben! Come downstairs!"

Ben **sighed**. He went downstairs to the dining room. He **started** to say: "I'm not hungry, mum. I don't want any lunch." But then he stopped. What was that on the table? It was a **parcel**. Was it a **present**? For him?

From: The Learn English Activity Book for Children

CATEGORIES

WRITE DOWN 3:

1. School subjects
2. Small pets
3. Nice things to eat
4. Languages
5. Books in English
6. Annoying things children in your class do
7. Sea animals
8. English songs
9. Plants
10. Horrible things to eat
11. Funny people
12. Nice things to do on holiday
13. Jobs you don't want to do when you grow up
14. Long English words
15. Sports
16. Vegetables
17. Things your parents can do that you can't do
18. Short English words
19. Countries
20. American movies

www.ingramcontent.com/pod-product-compliance
Lightning Source LLC
LaVergne TN
LVHW021741060526
838200LV00052B/3397